A Jigsaw Puzzle

poems by

Neil Craig Kennedy

Finishing Line Press
Georgetown, Kentucky

A Jigsaw Puzzle

ACKNOWLEDGMENTS

The following poems were first published by Origami Poems Project:

In May of 2019: Commuting cardinal; The wind is my guest;
Evening. You can feel; Having neglected; The folded blanket; Letting the
dog out; The muddy march snow; Look. Are those raindrops; Tell me when
you are done; The blue jays have told; You can see the creek; One of her old
socks.

In May of 2020: The tick of my watch; Pieces of puzzles; By the
kitchen stove; The clack of go stones; Behind the light switch; Around the
house; A little mountain; Lying on my back; The names and borders; Do not
be afraid; The comfortable, smooth; An upset basket.

In November of 2020: He gives her flowers; Board games on the
beach; A yellow jacket; Not waiting in line; Walking on one's own; Imagine.
Whose house; Outside the arcade; The car in the street; Girl on a park bench;
Play ukulele; The beach says nothing; The line for ice cream.

Publisher: Leah Huete de Maines
Editor: Christen Kincaid
Cover Art: Thomas Ranalli
Author Photo: Amber Kennedy
Cover Design: Elizabeth Maines McCleavy

Order online: www.finishinglinepress.com
also available on amazon.com

Author inquiries and mail orders:
Finishing Line Press
P. O. Box 1626
Georgetown, Kentucky 40324
U. S. A.

For my family, of course.

Flower on the floor.
Somebody has lost their bloom.
I am very careful.

After a long day at work,
The ignition key
Won't turn the engine.

Library night shift,
Eight ten. The books are quiet
And ready for bed.

Making all that noise,
Still dripping wet from practice,
The high school swim team.

Hanging a painting,
A nail falling to the floor
While I bruise the wall.

Oatmeal for breakfast.
My girlfriend wiping her mouth
Using my napkin.

The beach says nothing.
We argue on our blanket.
The beach says nothing.

Underpants and socks,
Shirts, pants, dresses, skirts,
Waiting patiently for you.

Students arguing
Over possible readings.
The book stays patient.

Our last night.
You separate our bodies,
The gentlest of surgeons.

She opens her book bag
Over the library desk,
Hands me an apple.

Girl on a park bench
Smiles and then looks away.
A shirtless runner.

The bird is missing his beak.
Picking up pieces.
A jigsaw puzzle.

The Cherry Orchard.
One of spring's greatest pleasures,
Tickets to Chekov.

The child delights,
Squishing ants in his fingers.
Small wordless people.

Spilling my coffee
All over the new sheets,
Your hand on my knee.

Finally learning
After years of pajamas
To sleep in nothing.

Writing a friend's name
The first time since their death,
Pen runs out of ink.

On my uncle's arms
Tattoos of angels
Decompose beneath the ground.

After the beating,
Officers in uniform
Talk of dignity.

Light from the hallway.
It's impossible to sleep.
Tell me a darkness.

A friend calls my name
The same instant you walk by.
I'm not listening.

What is it? Something
Flashes across a strange face
Too quickly for me.

Pearl Buck's typewriter
Receiving her visitors
In her long absence.

Open on the bed

The book of sonnets.

A night of worry.
Early morning trash truck sounds.
A sense of relief.

At the foot of the bed,
Even I've forgotten
The rubber mallet.

Theater lighting.
Almost time for the movie.
Theater darkness.

Clown Marionette
Laughing, resting on the head
Of another clown.

A phone going off
In the movie theater
On the movie screen.

Pick-up truck bumper
Confederate flag waving
"Save the whales" sticker

Opening the book,
Replacing the dried flower
With a new flower.

A virgin smiles
Compassionately
From a sinner's necklace.

Asking forgiveness
From a forgiveness machine.
Software malfunction.

Out of tune piano
Left on Wednesday morning's curb.
Garbage truck music.

Throwing glass against a wall,
Unsuccessfully
Timing a photo.

A hammer and a teacup
Go home together.
You might be surprised.

Do you think they'll come?
Each winter I want to die.
Then, the daffodils.

Martini glasses
A wine glass, a port wine glass
And a glass teacup.

Blossoming cherries
Show through the green leaves
Through the living room window.

Stained glass female saints.
The sound of something breaking.
Their congregation.

You can't fight progress.
Animals Humans Machines.
Moving in reverse.

Your mother singing,
Then not singing anymore.
Music history.

Funeral reading
Tennyson's *Crossing the Bar*
Funeral again

Setting the alarm,
Considering the mercy
Of other people.

Calling my sister
On the phone on her birthday
By our mother's name.

The sound of someone
Learning to play the cello
Avoiding practice.

Margaret Mead's old home.
Anthropology students
Talk about music.

Trump presidency.
By the immigrant's headstone:
American flag.

Driving the Chevy
Out of the fucking country
And finally home.

After reciting
Shakespeare's twenty-ninth sonnet,
Realizing I'm wrong.

You're reading Shakespeare.
My glass shall not persuade me—
Do you think I'm old?

Counting the money
Locking the register drawer
Turning the lights out

Calling an old friend.
Hoping she doesn't call back.
Answering the phone.

Watching teenagers,
Shocked to discover they take
The same risks we take.

An apple rotting
Still uneaten, all this time
In the bird feeder.

A cap-less acorn
Hidden in the boot's footprint,
Level with the ground.

It's spring. A bluebird
Flying out, then in, then out
Of a bluebird house.

Spring flowers travel
The distance between one color
And another.

A fighting couple
Call a momentary truce
To yell at the clerk.

Board games on the beach.
Stopping play to watch the sand
In the hourglass.

Tuning my guitar

The E string breaking.

Cleaning out my desk,
Finding the paper that held
Jessica's number.

An ex prison guard
Lifts up his binoculars,
Going bird watching.

Going for a walk
With nothing in my pockets
But my pocket watch.

Reading the paper,
Stepping over it
On the way to the driveway.

Paper acrobat
Feeding the paper lion.
A paper circus.

In the house, reading
Summer by Edith Wharton.
The snow keeps coming.

Mid-chess tournament
The power goes out,
The pieces now one color.

The last day of class.
Before leaving, the student
Steals a piece of chalk.

Robert Frost reading

Through the turn-table.

Leaving up the purple cross
Above my doorway
Until next April.

Nine in the morning,
Counting the bells from the church
As they ring ten times.

Ten in the morning,
Counting the bells from the church
Striking eleven.

After the stop sign

Right into traffic.

The spandex cyclist,
Waving to the police car,
Rolls through the stop sign.

A starling flying
Right out of Shakespeare's drama
To America.

English professor.
Epistemologically.
Misspelling the word.

Reading a haiku
About a profound silence,
My dog starts barking.

Saying the wrong thing
To the wrong person
The wrong way at the wrong time.

A woman my age
Walking her three dogs.
The other side of the fence.

Browsing the bookstore.
Placing *Medea*
On the Mother's Day display.

Talking to her,
The computer engineer,
About Greek drama.

English department meeting.
Two of the teachers
Whispering in French.

Too fucking tired
To finish making the bed,
But still making it.

On the bedroom wall:
The Virgin Mary
And a pin-up girl.

Trying, still trying
To untie the double knot.
Giving the hell up.

The robin returns
To find someone else's egg
In the nest.

In the morning, you find
The moon has forgotten
To close the windows.

Revealing the wall.
Rearranging the paintings
To fit the new one.

The rain gutter falls
Under the weight of the ice
After the snowfall.

Paint-drops on the floor.
White in the yellow bedroom.
Two colors ago.

Game pieces standing
On the library bookshelf.
The game board missing.

Piano music
From the house of the neighbors
I never speak to.

Hesitating clouds
Deciding whether or not
To cast a shadow.

A single bubble
Along the closed parade route.
Memorial day.

Come down here, oak tree.
Let us cold hungry people
Burn you to ashes.

Asking permission
To water the spring flowers,
The rain clouds rumble.

Breaching their contract,
This April, the daffodils
Open too early.

Not even asking,
The rain runs down our faces
And into our shirts.

Without a fire
These dusty fire alarms
Are growing anxious.

Removing herself,
Removing her undershirt
In the other room.

My shoes are racing
Each other down the hallway,
Both tied and untied.

Stop dancing so close
To the sand castle we've built.
Let's not ruin it.

Sunlight is running
Like warm water as it moves
Through the ice sculpture.

Construction outside.
My sink drain is a small door
For a centipede.

A tired coffee
Finds a spot to rest next to
A new computer.

Looking for the book
Last taken from the bookshelf
In your library.

Forgetting the place
I carefully selected
For my bookmark.

Dust from the flowers
Covers my car, turns it gold,
Makes the engine buzz.

(Expectation)
A robin hits my window
(And disillusion).

Pursued by a dog,
A squirrel runs through my yard
The long way around.

Half a blue eggshell
Is hidden between the gray
Cemetery stones.

My dog is surprised
To have found a tennis ball
On the tennis court.

A fat sparrow lands
On the greasy metal grate
Of a charcoal grill.

Sifting back and forth:
The sand in the hourglass,
The glass in the sand.

The comfortable, smooth
Heads of nails holding the hard
Wood floor together.

Water boiling
In a forgotten kettle,
Away and away.

Peeling an orange,
The sound of flesh stays longer
Underneath my nails.

Pulling back her hair,
The shoulder of her t-shirt
Revealing nothing.

Clean as fresh linen,
Undressing you before
Doing the laundry.

An upset basket
Spills fruit across the table.
Life is a still life.

Forgetting her name
In the memorial park,
I walk the footpath.

Pulling the lever.
Another coin in the slot.
Pulling the lever.

Washing the windows,
Artificial water rains
Quite convincingly.

Cleaning our bedroom.

The dirty darkness.

That huge starless sky.
On TV the detective
Solves the mystery.

TV news voices
Analyzing disasters.
A new pair of socks.

Museum hands touching
The featureless smooth surface
Of an angel's face.

Pouring the water
All over the tabletop,
Missing the glass.

Walking on paper,
My pen leaks through my pocket,
Leaving a dotted line.

Reading the dictionary

Running out of words.

After a shower,
Her hair still in the hairbrush
While she's off to work.

Tin cans and trash cans:
Wind turns over in the street,
Clattering them both.

Outside the circle
Of light, another circle
Of light: fireflies.

A naked woman
Is hiding in the garden,
Made of fresh marble.

Pieces of paper
Changing color over time
On a tree of words.

Absently humming
Jesus loves me this I know
In a parking lot.

Nobody stops me
Crinkling candy wrappers
After the movie.

Slowly exploring
The blanket chest of photos
Over the winter.

With a siren's song,
Calling young men to their deaths:
The fire whistle.

Her lips on my lips,
My wife secretly slips me
A mouthful of cake.

In from the garden
Washing the dirt from my hands,
There's mud in the sink.

One hundred dollars
Hidden inside a bible.
Snakes in the garden.

Sucking on a pen,
Mouthfuls of unwritten words
Staining my tongue black.

Do not be afraid,
I say to my alarm clock.
The alarm still sounds.

Opening windows,
My neighbor across the street
Listens to music.

Lying on my back.
The Sistine chapel ceiling
On television.

The names and borders
Have faded from the surface
Of my plastic globe.

The woman who walks
Across the bridge everyday
Did not cross today.

Car engines sputter.
The friction of my good shoes
Against the sidewalk.

A tumbler in hand.
Stars swept into the dust pan.
Then trash in the trash.

Going back to bed.
Waking up a second time
On Easter morning.

Just one chickadee
Has chosen to move into
Both my birdhouses.

Behind one man's voice

Another man's voice.

Inside of my name
On my high school diploma,
My grandfather's name.

A little girl hides
Beneath the blue canopy
Of her mother's skirt.

One watermelon
has burst open in the bin
Of watermelons.

Slow down, tomatoes.
The bell peppers are still green.
It's not a contest.

Letting the dog in,
Before I get up the stairs
There's mud on the couch.

Looking like a cat,
A small fox pauses, then slinks
Into the dog park.

Outlined in the dirt,
Underneath the welcome mat,
The shape of a key.

Washing the cement,
I remember the red line
Where the barn once stood.

My neighbor's hostas
Have done especially well
In my yard this year.

The double rainbow
Is too high. It might get struck
By the late lightening.

Recorded bird calls
Frighten the real birds away
From the blueberries.

I bet if you flipped
Over one of those gray stones
You would find a newt.

A piece of a snake
Turns into a length of rope
About the footpath.

Butter from my toast:
An open yellow window
On my kitchen floor.

The card catalog
Sits with one drawer half open
Deep in the junkyard.

Comic book pages
Turn on October sidewalks,
Fallen from backpacks.

Bright red and yellow
Prizes from the claw machine
Clutter my black desk.

One player wipes grease
From his hands before picking
Up his bowling ball.

The repair man saves
Some fallen terra cotta
From the warm furnace.

Boxes of used books,
Not speaking to one another,
Wait for the book sale.

The car in the street
Sits waiting for bicycles
To pass before it.

The door is open
Even though I've brought
The wrong key with me.

My soda bottle
Doesn't fit the cup holders
In the theater.

The library closed.
The municipal meeting
Is still going on.

Play ukulele
In the park and discover
How quiet it is.

The clerk follows me
Browsing through the used book store
I've always bought from.

Cemetery trees
Shiver from the ghosts who touch
Their roots and their leaves.

In the checkout line,
The boy just in front of me
Opens his new toy.

All kinds of small sounds

Fall from the tall tree.

By the post office,
In a pile of brown leaves:
A white envelope.

Eating samosas,
The first name on my receipt
Spelled incorrectly.

In the autumn wind,
The old tree regains its shape.
Spring for a moment.

An old dog takes off
Across the yard for rabbits.
Grandmother smiles.

I dropped a flat rock
Against the concrete sidewalk
And chipped its black screen.

Fall leaves pile up
Around the old school building,
Empty as summer.

That part of the trail
Is marked: Private Property.
But my dog can't read.

Back to the toy store.
Returning toys I bought
A summer too late.

Imagine. Whose house
Sits on that corner, watching
The beach and the ocean?

Air conditioners
Covered in plastic and tape
Are ready for fall.

Forget Christmas lights.
Every house on this long street
Is covered in snow.

The root beer fizzes
Over vanilla ice cream.
My small children squeal.

Lunchtime. A woman
Hands her son dishes and knives
To set the table.

On a sunny day
The doors to the storm cellar
Keep the shadows dry.

A porcelain bird
Nesting on the reference desk
Never gets startled.

My sister moving
Between each headstone, leaving
Piles of birdseed.

I've left a corner
Of grass uncut in the yard
For the neighbor's cat.

Three cups are posing
On the kitchen countertop:
Tea and wine and milk.

Looking up the word
She asked me to spell for her
In her dictionary.

The bottle of wine
For my twenty-first birthday
Went bad unopened.

I stole those two stones
Intended to have held down
The picnic basket.

The young boy smiles,
Playing with green army men
On a marble nude.

Who knows what's hidden

In the sugar bowl?

A little mountain
Of dirty laundry in this
Domestic landscape.

Kids make a collage
On the first day of advent,
Paper flames burning.

Tying my laces,
One shoe always takes longer.
Today, it's the left.

Gold olive oil
Holds bits of crust and breadcrumbs
On its soft surface.

Burning more slowly,
The candle is staying up
To see the new year.

A closed hay flower
And the open hay flower
Growing just beside.

The spider I've trapped
Under a glass waits for me
To open the door.

Surviving the crash
Of the vase against the floor:
A single flower.

My high-school notebook,
The name of an old crush
Inside the cover.

Not touching the tea
In the mug my friend's daughter
Usually drinks from.

My kitchen counter
Has been dusted with flour,
Waits for finger prints.

Around the house,
Empty glasses of water
Tell me where she's been.

As she hands me the money
The old woman's nails
Are painted bright gold.

During the blackout,
An oil lamp is burning
On a black table.

One of the four chairs
Is replaced at the table
By a wooden stool.

That big maple tree,
Hero of my childhood,
Was cut down today.

A yellow jacket,
Surprising the picnicker,
Leaves the soda can.

A bed with blue sheets.
The wooden desk beside it,
Under the window.

Crickets are growing
Bigger than I've ever seen
In my warm basement.

Cutting vegetables
On my dad's old butcher block
In my mom's kitchen.

Two deer are prancing
On the field where little league
Meets every summer.

The name of a girl
(in a book from the thrift store)
I went to school with.

Balled up and hidden
Down in the laundry basket:
A pair of boxers.

The smell of new spring.
Everyone I have lied to
Somehow believed me.

I didn't expect
To meet you, little Jesus,
In this gas station.

How could we have known,
Flying a kite on the beach,
Dad was filming us?

Talking about time
Over tea with my mother.
The cookies go stale.

Collected poems
Can be ripped out of their book
And left here and there.

A siren follows
Some disaster down the street.
I scratch my left foot.

Shadows extending
Under a low yellow sun:
My life grows longer.

After the farm hand
Has finished grafting a branch,
The tree wears a cast.

Not noticing me,
She hums a tune to herself,
Shuffling papers.

Smell the hot water
Running through the old baseboards
And heating the house.

Escaping his desk,
The boy stares out the window,
Sharpens his pencil.

The owners have left.
Outside the closed-up store front,
One statue hangs out.

Up the attic stairs
To find the plastic snowman
For the living room.

It's a tradition:
Shattering the ornaments
For the Christmas tree.

I should be careful,
Having left a clothes hanger
On my bed all day.

I should be careful,
Having let the water run
In the sink all day.

Locked in my bedroom,
My dog pushes newspaper
Squares under my door.

A little Atlas,
My daughter picks up the globe
I've just knocked over.

Pushing snow off my windshield,
My new ice-scraper
Safe inside the house.

Behind the light switch,
The last person to wire
Those wires is gone.

I never get bored
Of turning the hands
Of my watch ahead and back.

Salting the driveway,
He stops and takes off his gloves
To blow on his hands.

It lasted longer
Than the candles from the store:
One my mother made.

The boxwood has caught
A branch the oak discarded
In the storm last night.

Holding them up to my eyes:
Half drinking glasses,
Half binoculars.

Jesus on the cross
Hangs next to the thermostat
on a yellow wall.

The clack of *go* stones
On wood mixes with the sound
Of the sink dripping.

Having neglected
To shovel my own sidewalk,
I stroll through the town.

Doodles on the desk
Listen most attentively
To the class lecture.

Commuting cardinal,
Streak the blood of your body
Though this subway car.

Tell me when you're done.
I'll throw you a funeral,
Potted daffodils.

Take apart this chair
Your father used to sit on.
Put it on the curb.

An empty trash can
Pauses while crossing the street
On a windy day.

Ash from the incense
On the mantle. On the floor,
Ash from the fire.

The folded blanket
Over the arm of the chair
Is keeping it warm.

Evening. You can feel
The cold of the hardwood floor
Inside your socks.

The wind is my guest.
It climbs in through the window,
Ignoring the door.

How the clouds don't move
And then, for no reason, do:
There should be a word.

By the kitchen stove,
Bottles of olive oil
Hold olive oil.

The blue jays have told
The other birds in the woods
Their guests have arrived.

How that kite thrashes!
Its tail string is all tangled
On a broken bough.

In a restaurant,
A couple eat their dessert
At separate tables.

After my son's fall,
The white sidewalk shows no sign
Of blood from his knee.

One of her old socks,
Folded in the comforter
At least since winter.

Little beads of ice
Everywhere on the branches
Of the dogwood tree.

You can see the creek
Through these trees in the winter
When their leaves are gone.

Nine-year-old witches
Laugh over cups of cider.
Almost November.

A few friends drink
Leaning against the brick wall.
No room at the bar.

Oh this stubborn blind
Won't stay down where I pull it.
It's nice out tonight.

The only star out
Is somehow aligned
With the top of the fir tree.

Pieces of puzzles
Mixed up in their boxes
From summers ago.

The muddy march snow.
The bridge over the canal
Has been repainted.

Look. Are those raindrops
Or is the ice just melting
From yesterday's snow?

My shadow mixes
Like a part of the forest
With those of the trees.

Letting the dog out,
She hesitates at the door,
Surprised to see snow.

On a perfect day
The wind through a judas tree
Makes it rain flowers.

The sound of sweeping
From the floor below me
Stirs up the dust.

Discarding some books,
The wall behind the bookshelf
Appears on the shelves.

Bundled in a rubber band,
The daffodil bulbs
Wait for next winter.

Not even dark yet,
And the cats have already
Come out for the night.

Late for the school play,
A scarecrow hops from the car
And runs up the steps.

Two brown mergansers
Slowly making their way through
The flock of mallards.

The tick of my watch
Becomes louder when I place it
Face down on my desk.

Brown leaves cover up
The entrance to the burrow.
My dog doesn't mind.

A black vulture waits
By the edge of the thicket.
The smell of something dying.

Mr. Blue Heron
Carefully keeps a tally
Of fish in the pond.

Behind the counter
The woman sits up straighter,
Noticing I'm here.

The flowers shatter.

The vase stays intact.

Sweeping out the leaves
That have blown under the closed
Door of my garage.

The man carries his guitar
Up the outside steps
To his apartment.

Since they leveled the pavement
Rain pools in the street.

Walking on one's own.
Conversation samples pass
By on the boardwalk.

Outside the arcade,
The kids get up to a game
Of paper football.

There's snow on the beach,
Snow drifts looking like sand dunes,
The ocean the same.

Not waiting in line,
Kids covet the gelato,
Hands against the glass.

He gives her flowers
On the beach. They plant roses
In the sand.

The line for ice cream.
The moon touches the ocean.
The length of the year.

Prior work:

"If you Can't Love an Ordinary Bird." Friend's Journal. May 2021.

"The Red Upon the Wing." Right Hand Pointing. April 2021.

"Rain Forms Rivers." Right Hand Pointing. April 2021.

"Cubism." Better Than Starbucks. February 2021.

"Upon Seeing the Death Mask of John Keats…" The Orchards. December 2020.

"We Shredded Books on the Library Floor." 805 Lit + Art. December 2020.

"The More or Less Convicted." The Road Not Taken. Fall 2020.

The Beach Says Nothing. Origami Poetry Project. Fall 2020.

"All Day After the Morning Our Dog Caught." Best of Kindness 2020. Origami Poetry Project. Fall 2020.

"Cicadas." One Sentence Poems. August 2020.

Tiny House Poems. Origami Poetry Project. Spring 2020.

"How Airplanes Stay Up." Better Than Starbucks. March 2020.

"Sloshing and Grumbling." One Sentence Poems. January 2020.

"When Juliet." The Orchards. Winter 2019.

"Nicole." The Road Not Taken. Summer 2019.

Ignoring the Door. Origami Poetry Project. Spring 2019.

Neil Craig Kennedy is a poet and librarian. He holds an AA in Liberal Arts, a BA in English Literature, an MFA in Creative Writing, and an MS in Library Science. He lives outside Philadelphia.

www.ingramcontent.com/pod-product-compliance
Lightning Source LLC
Chambersburg PA
CBHW031220090426
42740CB00009B/1246